Truth's Truth

Poetic Portraits

Truth’s Truth

Poetic Portraits

by

Joseph Kleponis

Cover design by Shay Culligan
Author photo courtesy of
@angelarowlingsphotography

ISBN: 978-1-954353-42-8

Kelsay Books
502 South 1040 East, A-119
American Fork, Utah, 84003

Dedicated to Ileana who listens and encourages.

Special thanks to Angela Rowlings, J.B. and others, who offered input as this manuscript took shape.

Acknowledgments

The author wishes to acknowledge the editors of the following publications in which these poems appeared, some in slightly different versions:

Eucalypt: "In the Park" as "old men on benches"
First Literary Review East: "Winter Still Life: Hampton, NH," "Your Music"
Lawrence Eagle Tribune: "Spring Vision"
Magnapoets: "Crossing Fiedler Footbridge," "To My Friends"
Methuen Life: "Social Distancing"
Modern English Tanka: "Improbable Feats,"
Muddy River Poetry Review: "Daily Games," "Louie's," "The Quarries," "Vinny Criss's Teeth"
Pendemics Journal: "Still Life in the Time of Virus"
Ribbons: Journal of Tanka Society of America: "The Juggler"
The Aurorean: "Portrait of Improvisation," "What Relief"
The Ekphrastic Review: "Piano Notes and Dance"
The Leaflet: Journal of the New England Association of Teachers of English:"A Still Life: Frozen Afternoon," "Portrait in Blues"
The Penmen Review of Southern New Hampshire University "Duets of Violence in the Park," "Ode to the Merrimack River," "The Big Dig"

Contents

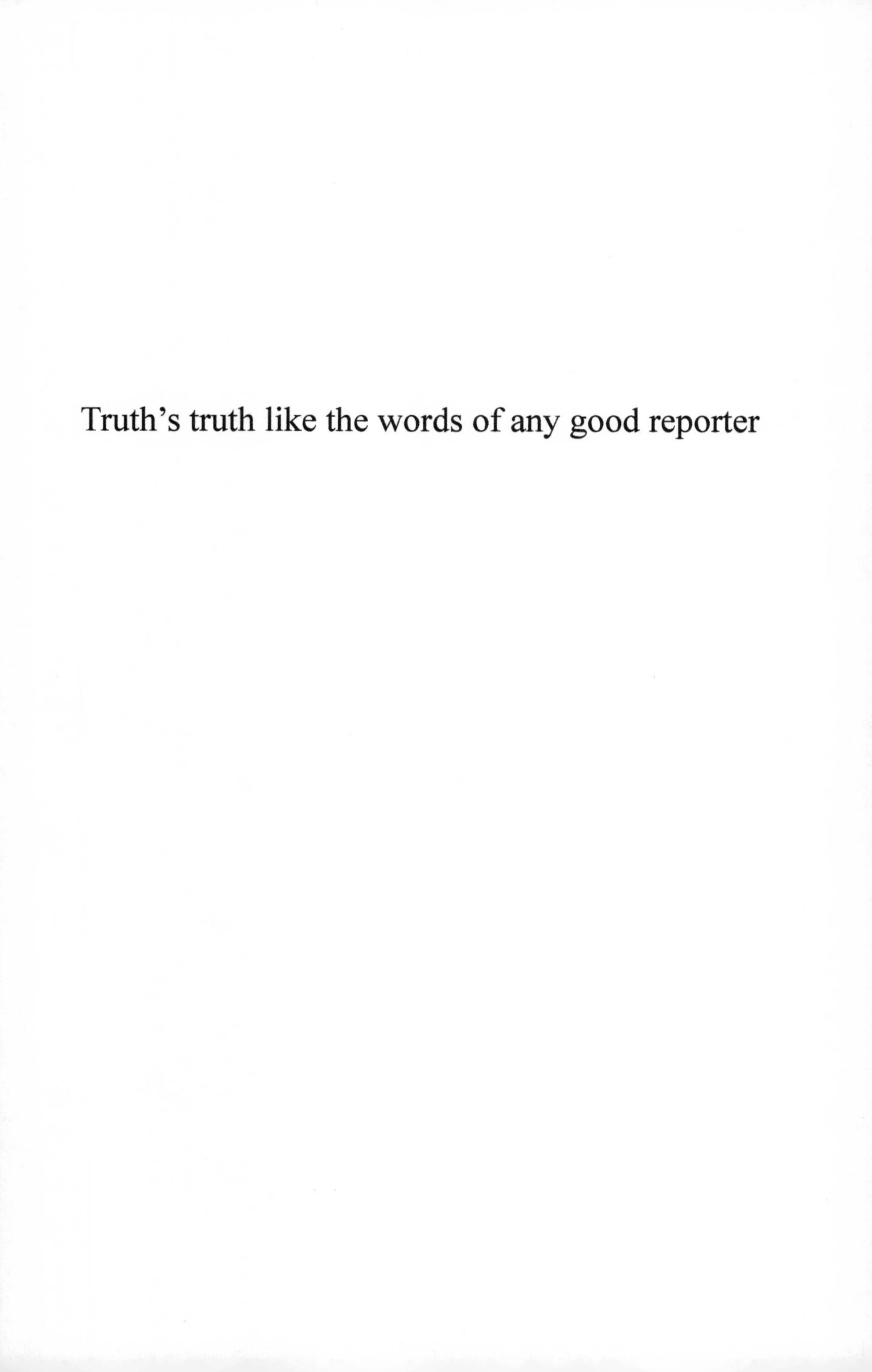
Truth's truth like the words of any good reporter

Vinny Criss's Teeth

History has truth, and so has legend.
—Victor Hugo

From the Arborway
to the Charles River or the Dedham Line
everyone passing the corner
of Lesher and Washington,
whether on foot,
or by car, truck, taxi, bicycle, or bus,
has seen it.

White against brick's blood red
a simple legend:
"Vinny Criss
has no teeth."

For over forty years
Vinny's toothlessness has been
a matter of public record.

But who is this Vinny Criss?
Why does he have no teeth?
Is the statement literal?
Is he a man who cannot eat a steak?
Or, is the statement figurative?
Is he a man with no bite, no juice, no influence?

Who wrote this statement?
Teenagers insulting an old man?
Rival gang members issuing a warning?
An angry, disappointed, bitter
fiancée, wife, would be lover,
sorry they ever got entangled
with a will-less toothless man?

Or, is it merely a simple statement of fact,
letting us know, that now and always,
Vinny will be pureeing his lunch?

Regardless of intent,
Vinny's toothlessness remains
and his story grows:

"He was a golden glover."
"He came home stinkin' drunk, and
his wife whacked him with a wooden spoon."
"He caught a baseball with his mouth."
"He fell out of a chair and kissed the table edge."

Our lives progress;
we graduate, marry, raise families;
we migrate from job to job
and leave the old neighborhood
only to return for a brief visit—

But through it all,
on the wall of a vacant store,
there is one constant,
a legend, a legacy, an epitaph, an historical fact,
open to interpretation, dispute, and possible revision—
"Vinny Criss
has no teeth."

Bubba

He had a name
his parents gave him
when he was born,
and it was surely recorded
in city ledgers and church books, too,
when he was christened,
but we didn't know his name,
or if we did, we forgot it.

The teachers may have called him by his name,
but we didn't listen,
or it didn't register with us
like so much the teachers said.

Maybe his mother, grandmother,
or the lady next-door
called him by his name,
but we didn't hear it.

We called him Bubba
because his little sister
called him Bubba
because she couldn't say brother
and never said his name.

So he was known to all of us
only as Bubba.

We wanted him on our side
in baseball, basketball, or football
because he was big, strong, agile.
He helped us learn the games.
He watched over us.
He was, after all, *our Bubba.*

After high school, he joined the military,
where he surely had a name,
and they did not call him Private Bubba.
But we really do not know.
We heard he was stationed in Hawaii,
and we imagined Bubba surfing.
More recently it was reported he had retired
to Alabama, perhaps,
with his wife, Susie, and three kids:
Billy, Sue, and Ray.

The years have passed
and all of our hang-outs—
Louie's, the A&W, the Rialto—
are either gone or changed,
but their names remain
embedded in our memories,
cementing their identity,
like the name Bubba,
the name of our brother,
whose name we never knew.

Louie's

Louie's was the place to be.

In the morning
kids would stop
to spend pennies, nickels, dimes,
on licorice sticks, bubble gum, juju beads
that they would secret away
and surreptitiously break out
when the monotony of the school day
became too much to bear.

On the way home
anyone who had a penny left over
might slide in
for a candy, or if flush, a coke.

Later the older kids,
the high school kids,
and the junior high kids
who should have been high school kids,
would take over stools at the counter
and order vanilla cokes or frappes,
and the boys would smile at the girls,
who would smile at the boys,
who would feed nickels into the jukebox,
and everyone would sway to tunes
until afternoon lengthened
and it came time to go home.

Then, men returning from work
would stop in to buy a paper,
or a pack of smokes,

and whisper numbers to Louie,
who would take a pencil from behind his ear
and scribble in a notebook.

Yes, Louie's was the place to be,
until the neighborhood school
stopped being the neighborhood school,
and the high school closed,
and men stopped taking the bus
to and from work,
and Louie retired to Florida
selling his store
to an alphabetized conglomerate
that doesn't stock candy
and removed the stools at the counter
but sells the state-run lottery scratchies
to locals like Sal
who never left the neighborhood
and stop by
for Keno and stale coffee
and memories
that fade fainter each day.

The Quarries

During the summer,
when the heat hung heavy,
all we wanted was to be cool,
so we hiked to the quarries.

We were as oblivious to the stories
of the dangers of diving at the quarries
as we were oblivious to the history
of how the rock had been cut
and hauled to Charlestown
over a hundred years before
to build the Bunker Hill Monument.
The only history we cared about
was our history. The history we would make
diving and retelling stories of diving
at the quarries.

The water, giant basins
of rainwater and snow-melt,
fed by ground water springs,
was, we had heard,
cold, dark, and deep—
the surface so dense
clouds were not reflected in it
and what lay below was obscured.

Our perch and our launch was a ledge,
cut into the walls of granite
that rose in jagged angles
twenty feet or more
above the water.

Over one lip of the quarry,
tops of trees, still and green, rose skyward;
over another, the towers of the Hancock and the Pru
were barely visible
through summer's haze.

Like the men who had labored there,
purposefully cutting and shaping blocks of stone
for a historical monument,
we worked at cutting and shaping our legacy
as we surveyed and plotted
how we would leap outward,
flinging ourselves as far from the rocky edge
and as far into air as we could,
so we would land, in what we imagined,
was a spot of cold, wet, sweetness.

Even now, in memory,
like a dream, but not dream-like,
I can feel the exhilarating terror
of feet no longer on solid ground,
of hurtling out through the heat,
all an intoxicating blur,
and the knowledge,
the terrible knowledge,
that a decision, once made,
will unfold in the arc of its course
leading to denouement,
that unlike fixed monuments of stone
cut and shaped by willful men,
will take its own shape and form,
leaving its own impact.

Daily Games

In the summer before the summer
of jobs, cars, and girlfriends,
there was baseball—baseball every morning,
and every afternoon,
stretching into twilight.

Hot and sweaty, covered in infield's dust,
we played game after game, in heat and in humidity,
even when Edgar's simple cousin knew
"It's too hot to play baseball"
we played and played some more.

In centerfield, Ace would drift,
backward or forward, whatever was needed
to make an effortless catch.
Frenchie pounded fastball after fastball
until he learned a curve
that took us half a day to solve.

Richie, Dave, Ratso, Petey,
Johnny, Eddie, Steve-o and me,
along with others who floated in and out
hung out at the varsity diamond,
even though none of us would ever have
the talent the talented possessed.

We played on, oblivious of the obvious:
that games at some time have to end
called short by obligation or other interests.

We argued rules,
compared strategies,
and shared what passed for secrets.

Who knows what we learned,
if anything, on those summer days?

Baseball as a metaphor is a conceit
for poets, playwrights, and storytellers
spinning tales that cast
hitters as legendary strongmen,
pitchers as slayers of hubris and muscles,
coaches as wily judges of men and motivation.

We were just playing a game
in long days of heat—
learning the angles—
judging distances—
calculating when to take a chance—
trying our hardest not to be gamed
by the game within the game
that, for a summer, was daily life.

Truth's Truth

Most truths are so naked that people feel sorry for them and cover them up, at least a little bit.

—Edward R. Murrow

He was tougher
than any of the toughs
who thought the block was theirs.

It's whispered
that he's the reason
Vinny Criss has no teeth.

But nobody knows for sure.
I mean, what do we know
of those we see
even if we see them everyday?
We can only know
what our eyes can see;
what we hear is only hearsay.
But before speculation of truth's truth
entered this discourse,
I was telling you about Albie.

He always had a day or two's growth of stubble.
Wild hair jutted from under a skally cap.
Dark eyes searched up and down the block.
Tatts of crosses highlighted his knuckles
before tattoos were de rigueur.
His black leather jacket
seemed to twitch as he moved.
And he smoked, unfiltered, of course,
and when he was done with a smoke

he'd flick the butt end with a stubby finger,
and the butt would sail end over end
in a glowing arc
into Washington Street.

Albie usually sat outside Frankie's Variety,
except when it rained or snowed,
then he sat at the window, watching, waiting, I suppose.
Kids never congregated on the corners
when Albie was on the prowl.
But he never bothered the little ones
who went to Frankie's for candy
or a loaf of bread. And, it's said,
he was respectful of the women
running an errand at Frankie's
or Frankie's brother's butcher shop
which was next door.

He was so good, he was almost
a cliché.

And we saw him watch the men
who got off the bus returning from work
and bought newspapers from Frankie
and who whispered a few quiet words
as they slid money across the counter.

Then, one day, we noticed Albie wasn't there.
A day grew to two, three, a week, a month,
and rumors that I'll not repeat here flew.

Soon, within a month or so,
Frankie's Variety Store closed;
Frankie's brother's butcher shop
was shuttered, too, and the block was empty
except for the pretend toughs who took to the corners.

No one knows where Albie went.
Someone said they saw
Frankie and Frankie's brother
sunning on a beach in Pennsacola.
I can only tell you what I've seen:
The stores on the block are vacant now,
weeds fill the alley between the variety store
and the butcher shop. And some one wrote
Vinny Criss.
has no teeth.
on the side of a vacant building.

Oh, I could tell you what *I think*
happened to Albie. But that would be speculation,
and this spectator can only tell what he's seen:
Truth's truth like the words of any good reporter.

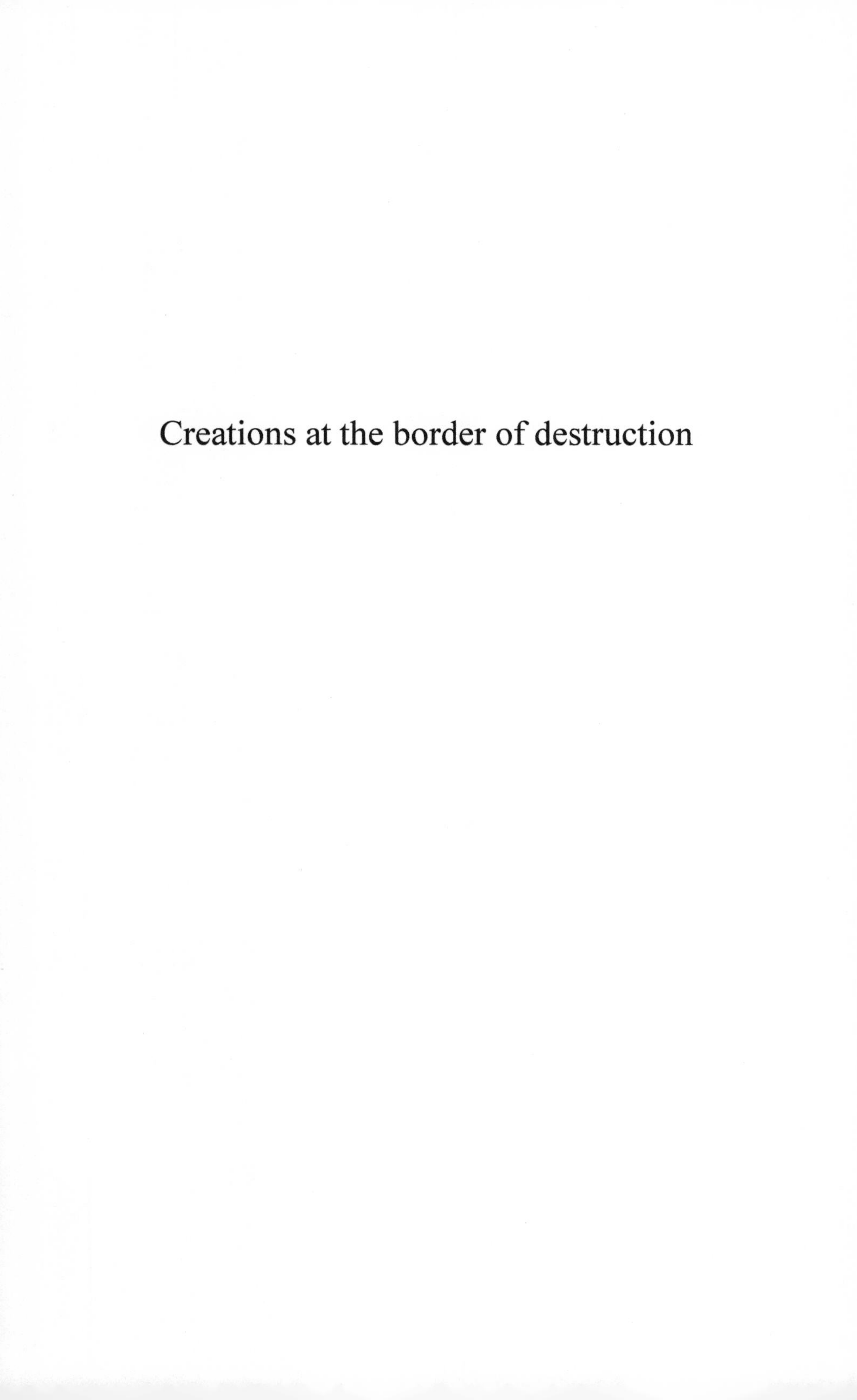

Creations at the border of destruction

Afternoon Lassitude

There's been three days of steady rain
while on holiday at this inn
with a balcony view
of a deserted beach.

The sky is the rain
that is the ocean
breaking monotonously
on the shore.

It's turned into another rum soaked afternoon,
salsa staining my shirt,
punctuation marks of afternoon's lassitude,
before the break for the Early Bird
at the jetport diner.

Will a rubber of whist
or the wail of a greasy tango
bring us blessed relief?

Portrait of Improvisation

Stepping to the edge of the stage,
eyes closed,
neck muscles straining,
sweat beading on forehead,
swaying into the bass's rhythm,
the tenor man blew notes:

> dawn's red fingers
> pushing through the edges of fading night;
>
> a new born babe,
> screaming for life;
>
> explosive creations
> at the border of destruction;

urging the crowd
to disavow its everyday life
and raise its soul on song's wing
and live!

Blue Tuesday Night Cliché

On a quiet night, a Tuesday night, say,
when you know there won't be another fare,
especially since ride sharing has killed your trade,
you really don't want to put up early
because the street is all yours to see—
the yellow lights from warm apartments,
the liquor store empty but glowing,
maybe somebody tottering homeward
a fifth of comfort under his arm—
the lullaby of tires on asphalt
if accompanied by a blue saxophone
would complete the cliché of your cliché—
and you know that tomorrow will be the same.

But this is a peaceful epiphany,
and you ride on in the quieting night
without anticipation,
the street all yours,
the night all yours as well,
to caress,
    to hold,
        to surrender to.

Baggage

battered
bruised
scarred
frayed

handled and mishandled

lost and found

labelled

cast aside
stored away
returned to use

showing:
    where we've been
    where we'll go
    who we were
    who we want to be

carrier of the essential and unessential

identifies
the essence of our essence.

Fumbling with our desires

Piano Notes and Dance

after Pierre Auguste Renoir's Dance at Bougival, *1883*

The piano notes are raindrops;
a flute is the breeze.
Her dress is layered white laces;
his suit is blue.
Her hand rests on his shoulder,
and his broad hand
encircles her waist.

They swirl—blue and white—
water and sky,
chromatic chords in a torrent.
Will their dance be longer than spring?

Improbable Feats

When you were three
you were a ballerina—
on tiptoe you reached
high over your head smiling
at your improbable feat.

Your Music

echoing crow calls
wind through dry leaves
sirens over rooftops
the el on a turn
sibilance
crescendo
decrescendo
dripping faucet
buzzing fly
promises and obligations
whispered words
of love

Duets of Violence in the Park

I

Two monarch butterflies
four orange, red and black wings,
violate tiny wild violets.

II

Two towheaded boys,
toy pistols in hand,
charge down the hillside.

III

Two milkweed seeds,
crazy lost snowflakes,
bend tips of blades of grass.

IV

Two jays,
jetting through the trees,
tangle over worms.

V

Two brown caterpillars,
dangling from a branch,
devour green leaves.

VI

Two lovers,
overturning their best friend's trust,
consummate a tryst.

Juggler

A street performer
coolly balanced on stilts
juggles cleavers—
such nonchalance is not ours
fumbling with our desires.

To fulfill dreams of adventure

Dreams of Adventure

On a summer morning,
just before the first light,
as the rest of the house sleeps,
the road calls to me once more;
the rush of tires on asphalt
carrying over the trees,
redolence of diesel
intermingling with wisteria.

Sound and scent suffuse my half sleep
and lead me to dreams of adventure
fueled by reminiscence of boyhood joy
found in unfolding a road map
and spreading it across the hood
of the family station wagon
and drawing my finger
along the red ribbon of road
that lead to the heart of the heart of America—
across the plains, over the Rockies,
to the winding roads of Big Sur,
toward California sunsets
and the expanse of the Pacific Ocean.

Gas was plentiful and cheap.
Detroit ruled the auto world.
America was safe and sure—
summer adventures easily planned
by looking at a map
from the local Esso
and following the arteries
that would pulse with cars,
surging from small town to big city,
connecting distant spaces
to fulfill dreams of adventure.

Now, even though the road calls,
it is only in this fitful early morning sleep.
The local gas station is shuttered.
There is no readily available map
to unfold and follow.
Summers are shortened by inevitable chores
and inescapable obligations
that are the fabric of life;
yet there is the yearning
to recapture the fleeting excitement
of whatever was lost
before the call to the road
became only a dream.

Ode to the Merrimack River

The Indians tell us of a beautiful river to the South, which they call the Merrimac.

—Pierre Du Gaust (c. 1605)

Merrimac, oh Merrimack,
"Swift water place,"
you are gentle and pure
as you tumble over rocks
at the confluence
of the Pemigewasset and Winnespasaukee.

Wending over hills and cascading
through forest falls and streams,
a place of abundant fish,
you fed the ancient Algonquins
before rushing downstream
at Amoskeag Falls.

There, at Manchester,
the waters of Thoreau
become wider and swifter yet;
inviting settlers to the banks
at Lowell, Lawrence, and Haverhill,
promising to sustain their lives.

In those cities of brick and stone,
the homes of Kerouac and Dubus
who paid homage to your pulse,
Man straightened you,
and bent you, turned you—
using your power for his purpose—

Boott Cotton Mill, American Woolen,
countless shoe shops
producing goods;
the commerce flowing from you
along the Middlesex Canal
to Boston and beyond.

Your waters
no longer so pure—
fouled with dyes and other detritus—
Man, whom you nutured,
disgraced you
and subjugated you further still.

And so you flow within his bounds,
as if accepting his command,
until rain, snow, and ice
swell you to greatness once again
and urge you to press in a torrent
against those meager restraints.

Then you rage
past the cities, under the bridges, over the dams,
back-flooding distant tributaries
in Wilmington, Andover, or Amesbury—
showing your power once more.

At Newburyport,
where Samuel de Champlain
first set eyes on your shimmering waters,
boats are raised to escape your torrent;
and you rise in finality over Salisbury's black rocks—
to become forever free, joining the tides of the sea.

Poets can only tell the truth of images created by words

To My Friends

Your letters and phone calls,
exotic stamps and crackling wires,
find me from across continents and seas.

Magical dances,
flooded deltas rich at planting time,
a rhythmic bending and thrusting in the mud,
museums in Florence,
clacking prayer beads on Aegean Isles,
hazy vistas,
chicken killing at a kibbutz,
are your fields.

And I am here—still—
studying the American idiom:
my oak veneer dining room table,
my students' churlish sayings.

The sun sets behind trees,
their branches are burning fingers
reaching beyond—
but you've heard that line before,
so, what is there left for me to say?

As the circle of our circle
ever widens like a universe unto itself,
I am no fixed locus,
but a shifting point of reference
growing through the words of your love.

Spring Vision

Walking up Beech Path in Arnold Arboretum,
just below the crest of the hill,
before the city explodes into view,
in the rising hilltop meadow
I see the head of a purple crocus,
juxtaposed against the late snow
that is melting in early spring sun.

If I were Robert Frost
I'd speak of the fury of nature
caught in that moment:
simultaneous creation and destruction—
hope and unfulfilled promise—
nature's cyclical dance.

But I am not Robert Frost;
and I only see
a purple crocus
stark against white snow
that is melting in early spring sun.

Crossing Fiedler Footbridge

Cherry blossoms
like snowflakes
petal the still dark limbs
overarching the banks
of the Charles River Lagoon.

A worn, wooden gondola,
red, white, and green,
rocks like a misplaced toy
on the choppy surface
of the still icy waters.

In counterpoint to the rush of tires on asphalt,
honking geese rise in a splashing V
toward the fading afternoon sun.

Pausing before the silent Hatch Shell
I dream of the promise of summer's music,
before turning to cross the solid footbridge
back to the crush of crowded city streets.

And in that pausing
I think I believe
I have found
clarity,
for the moment,
anyway.

The Big Dig

The downtown stretch
of the Southeast Expressway
is underground now;
the North End and Downtown,
Financial District and Waterfront,
are connected, yet separated,
by the expanse
of the Rose Kennedy Greenway.

Of course, the older neighborhoods—
South Boston and Roxbury,
Dorchester and its other half—
are still cleaved
by the ironwork and asphalt
road of commerce
that was to keep the Hub
The Hub.

What this road
and its history
say about us—
our changing hopes and desires—
is perhaps, the work
of historians or archaeologists
who'll dig deeper
still—

For poets
can only tell the truth
of images created by words—
elusive and shifting—

like the shadow of day before night
or the sound of sound
rising
at dawn's half-light.

Our Sustenance

On a summer afternoon while at lunch
at a restaurant along the river,
we sat under a shading awning
sipping white wine paired with Romana salad.

We conversed about matters of the day—
the children, politics, our appointments.
We congratulated ourselves on the view:
the swift river coursing through this old city,
renovated red brick mills on its banks,
the water reflecting the sky's blueness,
when a bird swooped low
barely breaking the water's surface
and emerged with a fish clamped in its beak.
A ribbon of blood stained the writhing fish,
its silver scales shining in the light
as it frantically gulped the killing air.

Then, the bird, as I suppose only birds do,
pushed the fish under the water's surface
and re-emerged with it firm in its claws
riding the current and the fish downstream.

And we returned to our bread and our wine,
talk of daily events, our sustenance.

I see and hear this now,
and you do, too.

Morning Still Life

Morning light rains
through trees
and across a patch of daylilies.
A bird lights
on a branch
and lifts its head
singing.

I see and hear this now,
and you do, too;
and we endue this moment
with meaning,
although this morning still life
would still be life
regardless of what we do.

What Relief

The summer sun is a relentless torch,
the sidewalks a Sahara of cement
broken only by weeds poking through cracks.

At night, dead air presses downward
forcing broken smoke rings
from our cigarettes
back to the curb.

We can only imagine
that somewhere, far beyond here,
icy chips of stars illuminate the night
for others whom we cannot quite know.

Maybe those who sit next to blue cool pools
drinking night's delicious air
while looking to the heavens
do wish future wishes.

But we, on steamy front stoops,
stare at hydrants
or try to see above rooftops,
all the while wondering
what relief might come our way.

Winter: Hampton, NH

Ocean Boulevard is deserted now.
The sidewalks are gray and cold.

The Playland Arcade is shuttered for now—
no thumping skee balls or jangling pinballs
echo through this wind-swept afternoon.

The only sound's the faint crash of breakers

No scent of corn dogs, fried dough, or smoothies
rises through a coconut-oiled crowd
of tanned bodies shirtless or bikinied
noshing, and gawking, and flirting, and hoping
for fulfillment on a heated night.

There is only cold descending on cold,
and waves pummeling the sandy berm
and snowflakes falling one on one.

A Frozen Afternoon

The frozen river
gives back the city and the sky
in a clouded picture
of bricks, steel, and concrete.

Barren trees at the water's edge
sway in late afternoon's fading light;
walkers and runners
bundled in layers
struggle stiffly through the cold.

No ducks skim the waters,
and the boats are motionless now, too,
shrink-wrapped at their moorings;
waiting for that moment
when they'll be uncovered
and readied to push
through still shivering waters
toward the wider harbor.

For now, man and nature
are in unison, frozen,
waiting for warmth
and to move once again.

…not just another inning,
but of a chance to prevail

The Keno Players

During this pandemic spring
at the Johnny Convenience Store
the keno players
still sit in greenback chairs
at wood veneer tables
staring at a blue-gray screen
watching the numbers roll on—
chance, another name for statistics,
determining whether to live
another hour
or to fold and go home
to the unsettling quiet
and different dreams
of beating the odds.

Social Distancing

Stillness upon stillness still
broken only
by a woodpecker
tapping,
marking its territory.

Still Life in the Time of the Virus

There is the cliché
of rosy fingered dawn
pushing away
the curtains of night.

There is morning birdsong,
for me
but not for me.

There is the sky
perhaps no bluer than it has been
yet bluer still.

There are the church bells;
I heard them before;
I hear them again.

There are the walkers
walking together
but apart.

There are the neighbors
but not at the fence line.

There is a smudge in the trees,
crows staging
as evening calls.

There are the icy chips of stars
across the sky,
still indifferent from afar.

There is this stillness
an unusual stillness
that is now no longer new.

Our Crucible

Old Giles Corey would not submit.
It's said he cried, "More."
When he was pressed.
And so he was pressed more.
They added more weight,
stone upon stone on his chest
until he could no longer breathe.

In this season
of virulence and hate,
weight upon weight
bears down upon us,
until it is as if
we, like old Giles Corey,
will be crushed.

And so, we pray for relief,
change that will inoculate us
from the oppression of this crucible,
allowing us to breathe once more.

Not Just Another Inning

Chaos was the law of nature,
Order was the dream of man.
—Henry Adams

Locked within
in this spring of disorder
I retreat to the attic
to organize,
for solace
in the ritual of cleaning.

In a box in a corner
there's my catcher's mitt.
It's still supple,
the pocket worn, blackened
from receiving pitch after pitch:
  high heat,
  slow curve,
  change-up in the dirt.

From behind the plate
I called the shots—
pitcher and fielders
following my lead,
in my control.

Now I reach for something solid.

I hold the mitt close,
in the scent of leather
there's spring,
summer,
hopes and dreams,
of not just another inning,
but of a chance to prevail.

on feet that do not know the rhythm of this dance

Father's Garden

Family legend propagates the myth
that Father was a gardener,
that he cultivated vegetables
and flowers in our stony, city yard.

It's true he planted plants:
Row after crazy row of tomatoes,
both perfect and blighted,
beds of flowers: marigolds,
zinnias, mixed with dahlias and gladioli
as if scattered by the wind
or drunken birds.

Day after day, after work,
Father would stand in his yard
a three-cent cheroot or philly
clenched in his teeth
while he sprayed water
on flowers and vegetables
whether they needed it or not.

We knew not to disturb him,
that we, too, would be tended to
whether we needed the tending
or not.

Oh Mother, My Mother

our intricate dance of changing tempo
sometimes stopped our feet,
and we stumbled,
our hands not quite touching
as the lead changed
in our improvised steps
of unbalanced balancing.

Oh Mother, my young mother
of soft brown curls
and floral-patterned house dress,
you waited for me at the schoolyard gate,
taking my hand as I slipped from the line
of classmates. You walked me
past the drugstore, the barbershop,
the florist, and we stopped
at the Italian bakery where you bought bread
and let me carry the warm loaf home
where you sliced it,
and gave me milk, bread and jam,
while I told you the details of the details
of my day, and you nodded, you nodded.

And now as I tell you the details of life
beyond these walls, you nod and smile
until your face clouds, and you wave your hand
and you say, *"Take me home,
take me home."*

Oh Mother, my mother
of disappointed countenance,
what was it I did;
what was it I failed to do
so that our dance became a clumsy two step
of stumbling steps and almost falls?

Oh Mother, my mother
how your steps changed
as you leaned more on my hands
for what it was I could do
but could never do enough of.

Oh Mother, my tired mother,
in unsteady steps you fell,
and after they put your hip together
you lay in the hospital bed
swatting at my hand and softly singing,
"They grind the bones,
they grind the bones,
don't you know
they grind the bones."

Oh Mother, my broken mother,
your hand pushes me away
and reaches for me again
as if you cannot decide
if you want to be my mother.

Oh Mother, you who are no longer my mother,
you told them I had taken you to the roller rink,
and that you had held my hand
so you would not fall,
so you would not fall

as we skated in circles wider and wider
until you were tired and wanted to eat.
So, I took you to a restaurant
on the second floor with wide windows
where we could see treetops,
but the lunch, you said, was tasteless,
the other diners too loud,
the tv constantly blaring
so you cried, *"Take me home,*
take me home, take me home."
But I took you here instead
to wait, to wait, to wait.

Oh Mother, my poor mother,
what do I have left of you
but a woman who travels to places
she's never been,
who hears songs not sung,
who eats lunches never served,
who only sometimes knows my name,
who alternately holds and hits my hand
as the afternoon light fades into night.

Oh Mother, who is not my mother,
who will never again be my mother,
in the quiet of the soft white light
of the room that is your room
but not your room,
your hand circles in the air
and drops in mine, as you ask,
"Is it legal, can they do what they do,
is this night the night?"
And I say "Oh Mother, my mother,
It will be all right."

And I do not know
if that is the last you hear
from your son who is no longer your son.
And I leave the room in stumbling steps
on feet that do not know the rhythm of this dance.

The Restless Sons

We restless sons of the rooted sons
of rootless immigrants raced into the night,
eight cylinders of pistons throbbing
in oil-smoothed cases as we passed neon-lit strip malls
beyond the boundaries of our parents' milieu
headlong into the heart of American life.

The road ran narrow, and the road ran wide
from Michigan to Alligator Alley
and Provincetown to Santa Monica's piers,
our yearnings driving us onward
on the fevered route of go—gO—GO!

The day and the night were ours
to taste, to touch, to consume.

Unlike our fathers, whom we said *settled,*
we thought we had our forebear's spirit
as we rejected what was for what might be.

We journeyed, to find
ourselves, our lives, our futures,
restlessness a constant spur,
as we sought our essence
in the here and now;
denying we would ever stop,
not yet stricken by the realization
that like our fathers and our fathers' fathers,
we, too, are plagued by the undying want
to be free from the want of all want.

trying to devise strategies
to block the inevitable

The Cyclists

All of us, boys and girls,
even the kid with one leg in a brace
from polio, were bicycle riders.
Schwinns, Columbias,
three speed Raleighs,
beat hand-me downs, too,
some decked with colorful streamers
flowing from handlebars,
others with baseball cards
clothes-pinned to the frame,
fluttering *what, what, what*
from the spokes
as we pedaled faster
practicing tricks:
one hand,
no hands,
standing on the seat,
balancing a friend on the handlebars—
round and round
the neighborhood loop
pedaling to nowhere in particular
through spring and summer
into fall.

Now, on an early winter morning,
I, and men and women
I do not quite know
are bicyclists again.
Our bicycles
are a uniform dull gray.
The wheels whir as we pedal
to strengthen braced knees
and weakened hearts—
the pace for some is slow

and slower still—
the only trick we practice
on our stationary bikes
is pedaling on hopes
of the future.

In the Park

Old men on benches
rest in late winter sun
gathering warmth—
nearby a crocus pushes upward,
it too cannot wait for spring.

Other men, old chess players,
contemplate final moves
in the afternoon's fading light
trying to devise strategies
to block the inevitable.

About the Author

Joseph Kleponis, a retired teacher of English and American Literature, lives north of Boston, Massachusetts and reads with the Grey Court Poets. His poetry has been published in numerous journals including, *The Aurorean, Eucalypt, First Literary Review—East, Leaflet: The Journal of the New England Teachers of English, Penmen Review of Southern New Hampshire University, Methuen Life, Modern English Tanka, Muddy River Poetry Review,* and *Wilderness House Literary Review.*